Motor Racing

Tony Norman

Copyright © ticktock Entertainment Ltd 2006
First published in Great Britain in 2006 by ticktock Media Ltd,
Unit 2, Orchard Business Centre, North Farm Road,
Tunbridge Wells, Kent TN2 3XF

ISBN 1 86007 848 6

Printed in China

Picture credits (t=top; b=bottom; c=centre; l=left; r=right):
3, 5TL, 5CL,12B, 13T, 14B, 16B Shell; 8B, 9T,10B Autostock; 5 TR,
26-27 Chris Wright www.bangerracing.com; 19 Honda;
11T Mark Scott/Alamy; 21T Transtock Inc./Alamy; 4R, 5BR, 5BL, 7T,
18B, 21BL, 21BR, 22B U.S. Army

Every effort has been made to trace the copyright holders, and we
apologise in advance for any unintentional omissions. We would be
pleased to insert the appropriate acknowledgements in any subsequent
edition of this publication.

Contents

INTRODUCTION 4-5

NASCAR 6-7

ON THE TRACK 8-9

CARS AND DRIVERS 10-11

FORMULA 1 12-13

HIGH SPEED RACES 14-15

TEAM TACTICS 16-17

IN THE PITS 18-19

DRAG RACING 20-21

DRAGSTER CLASSES 22-23

DRAG CAR POWER 24-25

CRASH! 26-27

AROUND THE WORLD 28-29

GLOSSARY 30-31

INDEX 32

Introduction

People are passionate about motor racing. All over the world, people race cars. Some kinds are built specially for racing. Some look just like the cars you can see on the street. People even race beaten-up old cars, trucks and cars that look so funny they make you laugh.

BORN IN THE USA

NASCAR (National Association for Stock Car Auto Racing) and drag racing both began in the USA. NASCAR races are on fast tracks with high, sloping banks. Drag racing cars take off almost like rockets. Cars compete to reach the fastest speed on a 400 metre (quarter-mile) track.

RACING ACROSS THE WORLD

Formula One cars are single-seat racers. In 2005, 22 drivers from 14 countries raced at 19 different Grand Prix circuits all over the world.

There's not much space for the driver in a Formula One car.

FORMULA 1 FACTS - DID YOU KNOW?

Most of the controls and gauges for Formula One cars are on the steering wheel. Drivers find it quicker and safer to operate controls that are at their fingertips.

FORMULA 1

PIT CREW

DRAG CAR RACING

BANGER RACING

Drivers must wear helmets and fire-resistant clothes.

Race cars are often brightly coloured. It makes it easy for fans to pick out their favourite car.

NASCAR

NASCAR racing is one of the most popular sports in the US. The first **NASCAR** race was held near Charlotte, North Carolina in 1948. There are now more than 1,800 **NASCAR** events a year at tracks all over the US. One top event is the Daytona 500, held at the Daytona International Speedway in Florida every February.

The NASCAR rules state that all cars must be "American-made steel bodied passenger sedans."

DEVOTED FANS

NASCAR races draw huge crowds of more than 185,000 spectators, but this is only a small fraction of the number of fans. Millions of people follow the races on TV in the USA and in over 150 other countries.

THE RACES

The NASCAR race season lasts from February to November. The top event is the premier series, known as the Nextel Cup series after its sponsor. There is also the Busch Series for young drivers, and the Craftsman Truck Series for pick-up trucks.

NASCAR FACTS - DID YOU KNOW?

It takes 120 hours to build a racing engine for a Nextel Cup or Busch Series car. Mechanics spend 40 hours cleaning and tuning an engine after a race.

Daytona International Speedway
State: Florida
One circuit: 4 km (2.5 miles)

Greg Biffle won the 2005 Nextel race at the at the Texas Motor Speedway.

TRUE STORIES

Dale Earnhardt was one of NASCAR's best drivers. He had 76 careers wins, and he won on every major race track in America. Dale crashed and died in 2001 at the Daytona Speedway in Florida. His son, Dale Earnhardt Junior is now a top driver.

Bristol Motor
Speedway
State: Tennessee
One circuit: 0.8 km
(0.53 miles)

California
Speedway
State: California
One circuit: 3.2 km
(2 miles)

On the Track

There are 36 races in NASCAR's top competition, the Nextel Cup. Cars compete at racetracks all over the US. Tracks are all different lengths and shapes. Cars go round and round the track until the race has finished. Some races are 965 km (600 miles) long.

CHAMPIONSHIP POINT

The first driver in each race wins 180 points, the second 170 points and the third 165 points. Five points are given for leading a lap in a race. A five-point bonus is awarded for leading the most laps in a race. The champion is the driver who collects most points over all 36 races. The owners and manufacturers of cars are also awarded points.

IN THE GROOVE

'High groove' racers stay at the top of the slope to keep a steady speed and avoid slower cars. 'Low groove' drivers prefer to race a low line on the inside of the track.

Cars can reach speeds of more than 340 kph (212 mph).

All vehicles are inspected before a race to ensure they comply with NASCAR rules.

NASCAR FACTS - DID YOU KNOW?

Cars often drive nose-to-tail, just a few inches apart. The second car rides in the slipstream of the car in front. This is called 'drafting'.

Gateway International Raceway
State: Illinois
One circuit: 2 km (1.25 miles)

TRUE STORIES

Alabama 1997.
One of the biggest
NASCAR crashes of all
time happened at
Talladega racetrack,
involving 27 cars.
Many cars were written
off, but no drivers
were badly hurt.

Darlington
Raceway
State:
South Carolina
One circuit: 2.1 km
(1.36 miles)

Talladega
SuperSpeedway
State: Alabama
One circuit:
4.2 km (2.66
miles)

Cars and Drivers

When **NASCAR** racing began, competitors drove ordinary cars that had specially modified for racing. Now cars are specially built by experts for **NASCAR** races. It takes 10 days just to make the body from sheet metal.

Women NASCAR drivers are rare, but today there are a few that compete in the Craftsman Truck series.

TOP DRIVERS

Most NASCAR drivers wear full-face helmets which cover the head and face. These helmets weigh 1.3kg (3lb), but can feel five times heavier as the cars race round the steep banks of the track. Drivers wear seatbelts and have a head and neck support in case of crashes. Drivers must be in top physical shape to cope with the demands of the race.

TOP TEAMS

More than 30 teams take part in the Nextel Cup Series. Top teams may have five drivers racing for them during the season. Smaller teams have just one driver.

The Nextel All Star Challenge is only open to the winners from the current season and the season before.

NASCAR FACTS – DID YOU KNOW?

A car's power is measured by comparing it to a horse. NASCAR cars are rated 750 horsepower. That really does mean the power of 750 horses!

Memphis Motorsports Park
State: Tennessee
One circuit: 1.2 km (0.75 miles)

TRUE STORIES

Pocono Raceway, Pennsylvania 2003. NASCAR star racer Dale Jarrett had a lucky escape when his car crashed and burst into flames. Dale jumped out and ran to safety.

Kansas Speedway
State: Kansas
One circuit:
2.4 km (1.5 miles)

Texas Motor
Speedway
State: Texas
One circuit:
2.4 km
(1.5 miles)

Formula 1

The first Formula 1 World Championship race was at Silverstone, Northamptonshire in the UK, on 18 May 1950. There are now 19 races a year, held all over the world. A Formula 1 race is called a Grand Prix (French for grand prize). Grand Prix races are about 300 km (190 miles) long.

COST OF A CAR

It costs millions of dollars to design and build a Formula One car. Half this cost is for the design. Another big slice is for the engine. Other parts, like the steering wheel and driver's seat, cost thousands of dollars.

FEEL THE HEAT

F1 cars do not have a radiator cooling system. They are cooled by the air flow as they speed round the track. Races last about an hour and a half. Heat inside the car can hit 60°C (140°F). Drivers sweat off up to 5.4 kg (12 lb) in a Grand Prix. They drink through a plastic tube linked to their race helmet.

Successful overtaking requires powerful acceleration and skillful braking.

Drivers sit in the 'survival cell'. This must meet strict regulations to protect the driver in a crash.

FORMULA 1 FACTS - DID YOU KNOW?

Monaco is the only Grand Prix not to be run on a track. Cars race on the streets of Monte Carlo, which have many twists and turns and few chances to overtake.

Kuala Lumpa, Malaysia
One circuit:
5.5 km (3.4 miles)
No of laps: 56

TRUE STORIES

Dallas, Texas Grand Prix 1984.
UK driver Nigel Mansell ran out of petrol near the end of the race. Nigel tried to push the car over the finish line to win points but collapsed in the 42°C (108°F) heat.

Sao Paulo,
Brazil
One circuit: 4.3 km
(2.6 miles)
No of laps: 71

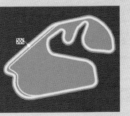

Melborne,
Australia
One circuit: 5.3 km
(3.2 miles)
No of laps: 58

High Speed Races

Formula One races are run on Grand Prix race tracks in countries all over the world. There are almost 50 circuits built to Grand Prix standards including nine in the US. Each race track has a different design, and each track is a different length.

STARTING GRID

The cars line up in rows, each with two cars. Lights on a stand above the track tell the drivers when to start. The day before each Grand Prix, drivers are timed round practice laps. The fastest driver goes to the front of the starting grid. This is called pole position.

HOW TO WIN

Pole position is good because drivers want to start in the lead. Overtaking is very difficult on most F1 tracks because of the many bends. Some drivers try to overtake when other cars slow down to go around a bend. It's very dangerous because the higher the speed, the harder it is to control the car.

The helmets worn by Grand Prix drivers have a supply of compressed air. Drivers breathe this if their car catches fire.

FORMULA 1 FACTS – DID YOU KNOW?

Zandvoort, The Netherlands, 1961. 15 cars started in the Dutch Grand Prix... and 15 cars finished. It's the only F1 event on record where no cars dropped out during the race.

Catalunya, Spain
One circuit:
4.6 km
(2.8 miles)
No of laps: 66

UNITED STATES GRAND PRIX
INDIANAPOLIS

21
22
23
24
25
26
27
28
29
30
31
32
33

CHAMPAGNE
MUMM

Cars leave the starting grid at the USA Grand Prix in Indianapolis.

The silver safety car moves in front of cars to stop them overtaking if there is a hazard on the track.

TRUE STORIES

Nurburgring Grand Prix, Germany 1976. Niki Lauda's car crashed and burst into flames. Niki was seriously hurt with burns to his head and broken bones. Despite his injuries, he was back racing just six weeks later.

Magny-Cours,
France
One circuit: 4.4 km
(2.7 miles)
No of laps: 70

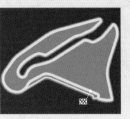

Silverstone,
UK
One circuit: 5.1 km
(3.1 miles)
No of laps: 60

Team Tactics

 Grand Prix drivers compete for their teams and for themselves. The winner of each race is awarded 10 points, plus 10 points for the team. The driver and team in second place get eight points, those in third place get six points. At the end of the season all the points are added up. The driver with the most points become world champion.

F1 cars are low to the ground to reduce the air turbulence (drag) that slows the car down.

TEAMS

Grand Prix racing teams are sponsored by big companies including motor manufacturers. Each team enters two cars in each race. Teams may have up to five different drivers. In 2005, 22 drivers from 14 different countries took part in the F1 season. There were 19 races.

DRIVERS

Drivers wear fireproof overalls, boots, gloves, underwear and balaclavas. They have straps on the shoulders of their overalls so safety teams can pull them out easily if there is a crash. Helmets weigh only 1.3kg (3lb) but are very strong. They have visors with layers of clear tear-off strips. Whenever one gets dirty, the driver can just tear it off.

The Brazilian driver Rubens Barrichello races for the Ferrari team.

FORMULA 1 FACTS - DID YOU KNOW?

Germany's Michael Schumacher was the first F1 driver to become world champion six times. He took the title in 1994, 1995, 2000, 2001, 2002, 2003 and 2004.

**Spa, Belgium
One circuit: 6.9 km
(4.2 miles)
No of laps: 44**

TRUE STORIES

Graham Hill was a F1 world champion. He died in 1975, just six months after retiring from motor racing. His son Damon became a Grand Prix star too, winning the world championship in 1996.

Montreal, Canada
One circuit: 4.3 km
(2.6 miles)
No of laps: 70

Indianapolis, USA
One circuit: 4.1 km
(2.5 miles)
No of laps: 73

In the Pits

NASCAR and F1 drivers all have their own team of mechanics. The mechanics work in a safe area by the track called the pits. Drivers use a two-way radio to keep in touch with the pits during a race.

An F1 car makes a pit stop to refuel.

NASCAR PITS

The Crew Chief leads the NASCAR pit crew. It takes a top pit crew less than 20 seconds to pump 83 litres (22 gallons) of fuel and change all four tyres. Tyre surfaces get so hot during a race that the rubber get tacky. This helps the car grip the track.

FORMULA 1 PITS

Formula One cars may only change a set of tyres if it rains. Cars average two pit stops per race to refuel. Two men are needed to pump fuel into the car at a rate of 12 litres (3 gallons) a second. Pit stops take an average of 6-12 seconds. An F1 car uses around 130 litres (35 gallons) of petrol in a race.

NASCAR teams are only allowed seven mechanics in the pits during a race.

RACING FACTS - DID YOU KNOW?

A racing car's black box is a computer that checks how the car is running, a bit like a black box in an aeroplane. It sends the information to the driver's team in the pits.

Many NASCAR and F1 flags have the same meaning.

HONDA

LOOK LEFT

LOOK RIGHT

BRAKES ON

ENEOS

LOOK LEFT

DON'T

WA

TRUE STORIES

Formula One teams spend over $2 million a year moving their racing cars round the world. The huge trucks used to carry the cars hold 380 litres (100 gallons) of fuel.

Race completed.

All cars must stop.

Danger ahead. Overtaking is not allowed.

Driver must stop at pits.

Drag Racing

Drag racing started on the dry lake beds of California in the 1930s. At first, dragsters were just street cars with parts of the body stripped away to make them go faster. They were nicknamed Hot Rods. The first legal races began in 1953.

Only two cars take part in each heat.

HOW THE RACE IS WON

The object of drag racing is to go as fast as possible over a short, straight course just 400 metres (one quarter of a mile) long. Two cars compete in each heat of a drag race. The winner of each heat goes into the next round of the contest. The last two cars left compete in the final.

OFFICIAL ORGANISATIONS

The National Hot Rod Association organises most of the drag racing events in northern America. Every year they run more than 5000 events at 140 tracks. The International Hot Rod Association has different rules from the NHRA. Most IHRA races are raced on tracks just 200 metres (one eighth of a mile) long.

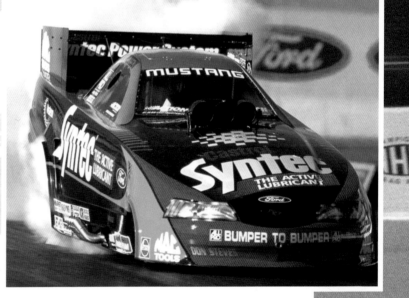

The top drag cars are specially built and can only be used on the track.

DRAG RACING FACTS - DID YOU KNOW?

A drag racer can accelerate from 0–480 kph (0–300 mph) in 4.5 second – that's faster than a jumbo jet.

The body of a Top Fuel drag car is long and thin to reduce air resistance.

TRUE STORIES

Top Fuel drag racing star Doug Kalitta from Michigan is also a skillful pilot. By the age of 21 he could fly a Lear jet – one of the youngest pilots ever to do this.

The brakes of a drag car produce so much heat that the tyres smoke.

The back wheels of a Top Fuel drag car wear out after only 4-6 races.

Dragster Classes

Over 200 kinds of vehicle are used in drag racing. Professional and amateurs all take part. Young drivers of 8-17 compete in Junior Dragsters races. Street Car races give fans a chance to race their own car on famous tracks.

Pro Stock cars are highly modified versions of models that are available to buy.

TOP THREE

Professional drag racing has three main classes.

Top Fuel Dragsters are the elite racers. They can cover 0–160 kilometres per hour (0–100 mph) in less than a second. In races, they can hit a top speed of 530 kph (330 mph).

Funny Cars are drag racers with brightly-coloured fibreglass bodies. Their big back wheels make them look funny. They can hit top speeds of more than 480 kph (300 mph).

Pro Stock cars look a bit like regular production model cars, but there's a difference. High-powered engines give them a top speed of more than 320 kph (200 mph).

The engine of a Top Fuel dragster is at the back of the car.

DRAG RACING FACTS - DID YOU KNOW?

Dragster engines are taken apart after every race and many of the parts are changed. The cost of one race for a Top Fuel dragster is up to $3,000 dollars.

Large back wheels make it look as if the body of a Funny Car is tilting forwards.

TRUE STORIES

Don Garlits is nicknamed drag racing's 'Big Daddy'. Don built 34 race cars, all called 'Swamp Rat'. He was the first man to top 402 kph (250 mph) and won 144 major events.

Funny Cars have rear-wheel drives with the engine at the front.

The engine of a Funny Car must conform to certain specifications.

Drag Car Power

All associations that organise drag car races have rules about how cars can be modified. The rules specify a car's weight, engine, brakes, body style and many other points. Many rules are there to keep the drivers, spectators and mechanics safe.

The body of a Funny Car covers the wheels to reduce air resistance.

FEEL THE POWER

Top Fuel dragsters have engines with over 8000 horsepower, 40 times the power of a family car. They run on a high power racing alcohol, not petrol. Dragsters use more than 37 litres (10 gallons) per race. Pit crew test fire the engines around 45 minutes before the race. The noise is deafening. Earplugs must be worn in the pits.

BURNOUT

Before a race, the car is driven to an area called the Burnout Box. Water is added to the tyres, usually with a spray. The driver applies the brakes and spins the tyres to warm them up. It's called a burnout because the tyres smoke. The burnout helps the tyres grip the track better.

Top Fuel cars use parachutes to slow them down after a race.

DRAG RACING FACTS - DID YOU KNOW?

NASCAR and Formula One ban fans from the pits during races. But drag racing fans can stand just feet away from the cars as pit crews work on them.

The lights of a Pro Stock car must be in the original factory position.

The air intake on the bonnet draws air into the engine.

Pro Stock cars must use special racing gasoline.

Crash!

Most racing cars are kept in great condition, with gleaming paintwork. But cars used in banger racing and demolition derby are old wrecks that are ready for the scrap heap. Both these sports are great fun to watch if you like plenty of crashes!

Banger cars crash into each other to try to stop rivals from reaching the finish line.

BANGER SAFETY

Banger racing began in the UK. The cars bang and crash into each other as they race around a track. Banger racing tracks are usually oval or shaped like the figure eight. The winner is the first car over the finishing line.

LAST ONE WINS

Demolition derby is big in the US. Cars do not race round a track – they just smash into each other in an arena. The last car still running at the end is the winner.

Demolition derbys are very muddy. The mud stops the cars from going too fast.

DEMOLITION DERBY FACTS - DID YOU KNOW?

It's not just cars that are used in demolition derby competitions. Fans also run events with tractors, school buses and even lawnmowers!

The many safety precautions mean that serious injuries are rare.

TRUE STORIES

England 2004. Banger drivers need luck. Kevin Chadwick's car was hit and smashed into a wall in the North West Open. Kevin came out with just a broken finger nail.

Most banger and demolition drivers are amateurs, racing just for fun.

All glass must be removed from demolition derby cars.

Around the World

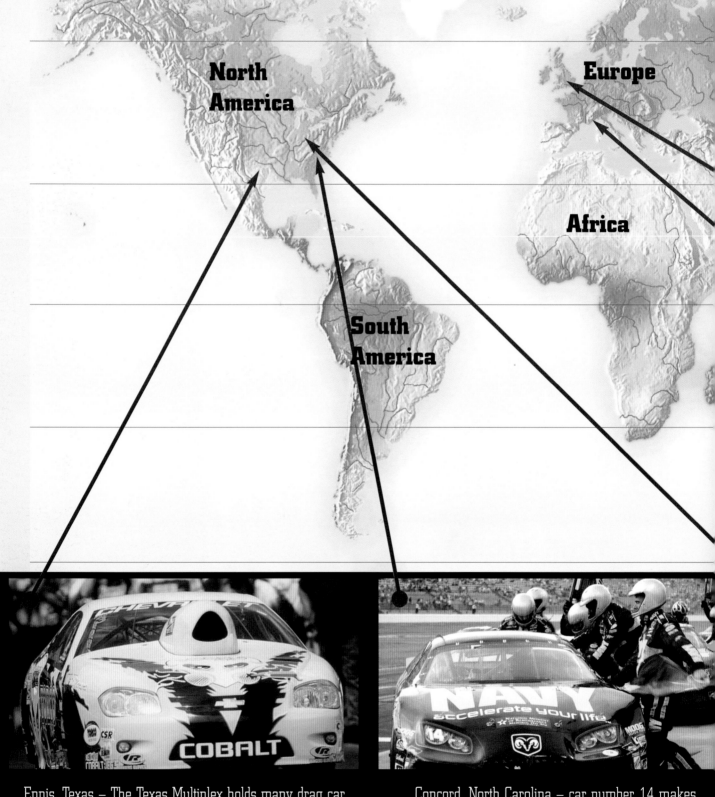

North
America

Europe

Africa

South
America

Ennis, Texas – The Texas Multiplex holds many drag car
racing events, including pro stock races

Concord, North Carolina – car number 14 makes
a pit stop at Lowe's Motor Speedway

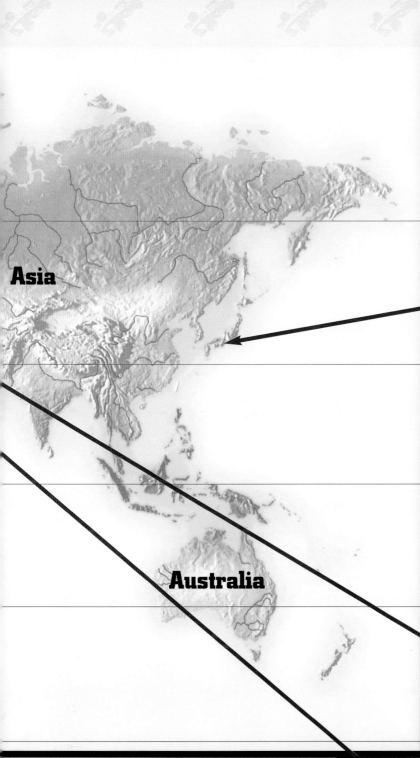

Asia

Australia

Suzuka, Japan - This top track has hosted the Japanese Formula 1 Grand Prix since 1987.

Silverstone, UK – First Formula One race held here. Still stages Grand Prix races.

Indiana, USA – 200,000 fans can watch races at the Indianapolis Motor Speedway.

Monte Carlo, Monaco - The only Formula One Grand Prix to be raced in city streets.

Glossary

Average speed
The number you get if you time every lap, then add all the times together and divide them by the number of laps raced.

Burnout
Spinning the wheels of a car to heat up the rubber so they run more smoothly on the track.

Championship
A big competition made up of lots of separate races The winner is called the champion.

Checkered
Patterned in squares of two colours, usually black and white. The checkered flag signals that the race is over.

Circuit
Another name for a race track.

Dragster
Another name for a drag racing car.

Elite
The best of its type.

Endurance
A type of motor racing in which cars compete for a long time, sometimes several days.

Event
In motor racing, a race meeting or competition.

Fibreglass
A very tough, lightweight man-made material which is often used for racing cars.

Formula One
A type of racing that uses single-seat racing cars in competitions at racetracks all over the world.

Funny car
A type of very fast drag car that has big back wheels.

Gasoline
A type of fuel used for vehicles of all kinds.

Grand Prix
A major race for fast racing cars. It means 'big prize' in French and gets its name because the first competition of this type was held in France.

Hazard
A danger.

Hot Rod
Another name for a drag racing car.

Horsepower
An amount of power equal to that produced by one horse before cars were invented.

Lap
One complete circuit of a racetrack.

Methanol
A type of fuel used for some car racing. It is safer than gasoline because it does not catch fire as easily if there is an accident.

NASCAR
National Association for Stock Car Auto Racing.

Nextel Cup series
The series of races the top NASCAR drivers compete in.

Pit
The area of a racetrack where cars go for tyre changes or repairs.

Pole position
The place at the front of the starting grid. The car that did best in the preliminary heats is given pole position to start the race.

Pro stock
A type of drag car modified from a production model (i.e. from a car that is available for ordinary members of the public to buy.)

Resistance
A type of force, especially the force produced by the wind pressing against a hard object like a car body.

Season
A period of time during which a series of events takes place.

Slipstream
The calm area behind a vehicle like a car or an aeroplane. Drivers sometimes like to tuck into the slipstream of another car to avoid the wind. It helps them to go faster or to use less fuel.

Spectators
People who go to watch events.

Starting grid
The place on the track where cars line up to start a race.

Streamlined
Designed in smooth lines so that the wind does not have any sharp edges to catch against.

Top Fuel
Name given to the fastest type of drag racer.

Visor
A clear panel at the front of a driver's helmet, made of tough protective material.

Index

A
acceleration 20
accidents 7, 9, 11, 27
air supply 14
average speed 30

B
Banger Racing 26–27
Barrichello, Rubens 16
Bernstein, Kenny and Brandon 25
black box 18
black flag 19
brakes 21, 24
Bristol Motor Speedway, Tennessee 7
burnout 30
Burnout Box 24
Busch Series 6

C
California Speedway State 7
cars 4, 10–11
cart 30
Catalunya, Spain 14
Chadwick, Kevin 27
championships 8, 16, 30
checkered flag 30
circuit 30
clothing 5, 16
colours 5
cooling systems 12
costs 12, 19, 22
Craftsman Truck Series 6, 10–11

D
Dallas, Texas 13
Darlington Raceway, South Carolina 9
Daytona International Speedway,
Florida 6–7
Demolition Derby 26–27
drafting 8
drag 17
drag racing 4, 20–25, 28
drinking 12
drivers 10–11, 16
Dutch Grand Prix 14

E
Earnhardt, Dale and Dale Jr 7
elite 30

endurance 30
engines 6, 12, 22–25
event 30

F
Ferrari 16
fibreglass 30
flags 18–19
Formula One 4, 12–19, 24, 29, 30
fuel 18, 24–25
Funny Cars 22–25

G
Garlits, Don 23
gasoline (petrol) 18, 25, 30
Gateway International Raceway,
Illinois 8
German Grand Prix 15
Grand Prix 4, 12–17, 29, 30

H
hazard 30
heat 12–13
helmets 5, 10, 14
'high groove' racers 8
high speed races 14–15
Hill, Graham and Damon 17
horsepower 10, 24, 30
Hot Rods 20, 30

I
IHRA see International Hot Rod
Association
Indianapolis, USA 17, 29
Indy car 30
International Hot Rod Association
(IHRA) 20

J
Japanese Formula One 29
Jarrett, Dale 11
Junior Dragsters 22

K
Kansas Speedway 11
Kuala Lumpa, Malaysia 12

L
lap 31
Lauda, Niki 15
Los Angeles, California 28
'low groove' racers 8

M
Magny-Cours, France 15
Mansell, Nigel 13
map 28–29
mechanics 6, 18
Melbourne, Australia 13
Memphis Motorsports Park,
Tennessee 10
methanol 31
money-making 6, 10
Monte Carlo, Monaco Grand 29
Montreal, Canada 17
mud 26

N
NASCAR (National Association for
Stock Car Auto Racing) 4, 6–11,
18–19, 24, 28
National Hot Rod Association
(NHRA) 20
Nextel All Star Challenge 10
Nextel Cup Series 6, 8, 10
NHRA see National Hot
Rod Association
noise 24

O
overtaking 13, 14–15

P
parachutes 24
petrol (gasoline) 18, 25, 30
pick-up trucks 6
pits 18–19, 24, 31
points systems 8, 16
pole position 14, 31
practice laps 14
Pro Stock cars 22, 24–25

R
racing alcohol 24
records 25

red flag 19
refuelling 18–19
resistance 24–25, 31
rules 6, 8, 24

S
safety car 15
Sao Paulo, Brazil 13
Schumacher, Michael 16
season 31
Silverstone, UK 12, 15, 29
slipstream 8, 31
souvenirs 6, 31
Spa, Belgium 16
spectators 6, 24, 31
speeds 8, 22
sponsorship 16
starting grid 14, 31
steering wheels 4
streamlined 31
Street Car races 22
Sukaka, Japan 29
survival cell 12
sweating 12

T
Talladega Superspeedway, Alabama 9
teams 16–17
Texas Motor Speedway 11
Top Fuel dragsters 20–21, 24–25, 31
tracks 8–9, 12–15, 26
tyres 18, 21, 24

U
USA Grand Prix 15

V
Valetta, Doug 21
visors 16, 31

W
women drivers 10–11

Y
yellow flag 19
young drivers 6, 22